The Impending Implosion of Cryptocurrency

written by

BENJAMIN BERGEN

BITCOIN DEFECT

Copyright © 2021 by Benjamin Bergen

ISBN: 9798735766407

First Edition – April 2021

Author Published

www.BitcoinDefect.com

Contact: author@BitcoinDefect.com

This book is provided for informational purposes only and is not to be taken as a replacement for professional investing advice.

All rights reserved. No part of this book may be reproduced or transmitted in any form or by any means without written permission from the author.

Foreword

Companies listed on major stock markets are required to file extensive paperwork before an initial public offering. They are also required to file annual reports. In the United States, this data is filed with the U.S. Securities and Exchange Commission (www.sec.gov) and is publicly available. Companies are legally required to list all their potential risks.

When it comes to "alternative investments" such as Bitcoin, there are usually still risks – albeit they may not have occurred to you or have been disclosed to you. This book aims to inform you of some of the risks of Bitcoin, which to some extent will also apply to other cryptocurrencies.

I approach this subject neither as an expert nor as an amateur. I have many years of experience in information technology, software development, and business management. This requires application of logic and seeing the broader picture. Others are more qualified to address blockchain technology, but many have incentives not to disclose vulnerabilities.

We live in an era when technology simplifies our lives in many ways, while making it more complex in other ways. There are nearly always pros and cons. With each convenience we gain, there is a downside. It may be thermostatically controlled electric heat, and then it quits in a power outage. Automobiles faster than horses, but then increased fatalities in accidents. It may be a remote-controlled garage door opener, and then the potential for thieves to gain access. Or email, but then getting a virus. Or it may be online banking, and then being hacked. A phone in our pocket, but then everyone expecting a response immediately. Almost everything has risks associated with it, and to nearly every advantage there is a potential disadvantage. Nearly everyone decides that these risks are worth the convenience, myself included. But with each convenience we adopt, we would be wise to consider the risks.

Table of Contents:

Chapter 1: A Currency Primer 7

Chapter 2: The Bitcoin Paragon 13

Chapter 3: Understanding Blockchain Technology 19

Chapter 4: The Software is Key 24

Chapter 5: The China Factor 30

Chapter 6: Environmental Impact 35

Chapter 7: Quantum Computing 40

Chapter 8: Traceability and Totalitarianism 45

Chapter 9: Prophetic Viewpoint 51

Chapter 10: Conclusion 55

Chapter 1: A Currency Primer

"Those who cannot remember the past are condemned to repeat it."

- *George Santayana*

The concept of cryptocurrencies, most notable of which is Bitcoin, is attractive for many reasons. Before we delve into this, a brief understanding of currency would be beneficial.

Down through history, we have seen currencies collapse or cease to be used. A couple millennia ago, the people of vast European empires used a Greek Stater or a Roman Denarius. But while such might have a collector value now, nobody is buying a new car or their groceries with these currencies of bygone eras.

Or a century ago, when after the first world war, in Germany due to hyperinflation it took a wheelbarrow of Deutsche Marks to purchase a loaf of bread. They literally printed extra zeros on top of existing currency to make it worth "something".

In more recent history, we have seen cases like Zimbabwe, where inflation has been estimated at over 600% in 2020, or a 2019 news report that stated: "Venezuela hyperinflation hits 10 million percent." Of course with such insane changes, there is conflicting stats and estimates, in part because it depends on what the inflation is based upon.

Whenever a central government controls a currency, they can produce more of it. A twenty-dollar bill has nearly zero intrinsic value. You cannot eat it. It does not even make a good notepad. But when a government designates it as "legal tender", businesses are legally required to accept it as payment for goods and services.

The value of our money is ultimately based on the trust of the people. When people stop trusting the government that produces the money – typically because the government is "printing" money faster than value is being added to the economy – the currency is devalued.

Money is all based on trust. When and while that shared trust exists, money is very convenient.

What is the alternative to money? Trading or bartering items of intrinsic value. You might repair the plumbing in my house in exchange for several chickens as payment. Or if you go to a restaurant to buy a burger, they might accept a sack of flour in exchange.

There are challenges with bartering, however. For one, we will likely have different ideas of what some item or some service is worth. Second, we might not want the items each other are offering. You might want what I have, but I have no use for what you are offering in return. Or I might want your service, but you have no use for what I am offering. Third, it is very inconvenient to conduct business while carrying chickens or a sack of flour.

Thus, thousands of years ago, the concept of money developed – where people agreed on various items having an assigned worth. Typically the items chosen were rare and difficult to obtain – such as precious metals like gold and silver. A certain weight of silver was accepted as the appropriate exchange for a day of work.

This was much more convenient, as you could carry in a pouch enough "value" to purchase a field or a house.

However, this was not a flawless system as a balance (the equivalent of a modern scale) was still required to weigh the silver or gold. And these balances could be setup fraudulently – either by not having the balance perfectly centered, or by having counterweights slightly lighter or heavier than what they were specified to be. As such, a buyer or seller could cheat on the payment. Furthermore, it was difficult to determine if the gold or silver had other less-valuable metals mixed into them, thus making them worth considerably less.

With the flaws and opportunity for fraud in such a system, when leaders came to power, they saw the opportunity to solve these problems for their people. They would mint coins of these metals – with stamped or engraved images on each side, and groves on the edges – thus making fraud difficult, as it was nearly impossible to shave some metal off without it being noticed, and difficult to create your own coins, thus nearly eliminating the concern of the metal being an alloy. And as these coins were of set weights / sizes / denominations – it eliminated the need for a balance to weigh the coins, thus providing a two-fold benefit – there was no more scale fraud, and not even a need for a scale; a farmer could now pay a laborer right in the field for his day's work with a coin that everyone trusted.

There was now a convenient, trusted currency with which commerce could flourish.

Nevertheless, eventually rulers realized that with the currency trusted, their coins could maintain trusted value while having them cost less to produce; they could make them slightly smaller, thinner, or contain less valuable metal.

Governments found they could even produce paper certificates that represented ownership of a certain amount of gold, and which could be traded to the government for the gold if desired. For large purchases, this was more convenient than carrying a heavy bag of coins.

Only the government could print these certificates, and anyone found to be counterfeiting them would be severely punished, and counterfeits would be destroyed.

Eventually people so seldomly traded the paper certificates for the gold it represented, as the paper currency was so convenient, that they stopped offering that option.

They later found that the people trusted this paper currency to such an extent, that they could remove the gold standard on which it was based – since only the government could print the money, there was a limited supply, and as long as it remained a trusted form of payment, everyone was satisfied.

Fast-forward a few years to the computer age, and rather than paper certificates, the money we mostly use comprises of digits on bank databases recording deposits and transactions. As long as the governments that issue the currencies limit the supply to be relative to the wealth generated in their country, generally the people trust the currency to have value, and the economy is stable.

What we see in cases like Venezuela, is that the government takes on levels of debt that it has no way to repay via collecting taxes. With its debt numerated in its own currency, it tries to "print" more currency to repay its debt, but this in turn leads to serious inflation, and in a snowball effect, the loss of trust in the government currency.

Granted, we are taking a simplistic view here – we have not dealt with loans, credit, interest, banks, and such. Money and finance have many nuances and complications; but all too often complicated factors cloud the simple and root basis of a subject.

In a later chapter we will look at some of these factors, but now with a better understanding of money, we can explore why Bitcoin appears to be an attractive alternative.

Chapter 2: The Bitcoin Paragon

"Success breeds complacency. Complacency breeds failure. Only the paranoid survive."

- *Andrew S. Grove*

With the concept of currency through history fresh in our minds, we will now explore the numerous reasons why cryptocurrencies, most notable of which is Bitcoin, are attractive, and have thus gained popularity in recent years.

From a **currency perspective**, there are several aspects that can be viewed as advantages of Bitcoin:

- No central government control
- No reliance on traditional banks
- Global scope
- Secure transmission
- User autonomy
- Finite supply

No central government control
The nature of Bitcoin is intended such that no single government has control over it. Being internet-based, and operating peer-to-peer, there is no "control lever" for Bitcoin that governments can manipulate, as they can with traditional currencies like the US Dollar, the UK Pound, the Euro, etc.

No reliance on traditional banks
Generally speaking, banks have a reputation of getting rich at their customer's expense. Besides the interest they make, traditional financial institutions are known for charging a multitude of fees.

Banks have certainly progressed in their technological approach, but they have a financial incentive to be slow. When wiring money or making bill payments, if they can hold your funds for even a day, that can represent significant interest opportunities for them.

Global Scope

As our economy becomes increasingly global, with goods produced in the most cost-effective locations around the globe, currency conversions become significant. Most businesses around the world have reason to deal in their local currency, and businesses in other countries thus need to have their local currency converted.

Secure transmission

The ability for two parties to securely exchange currency, regardless whether they are standing beside each other or thousands of miles apart, is not exclusive to Bitcoin, but when this can be done securely and in a matter of minutes without restrictions, it becomes more convenient than cash.

User autonomy

This is both an advantage and a disadvantage to Bitcoin. We will dive a little deeper into how Bitcoin and blockchain technology operate in the next chapter, but it results in a fairly anonymous transfer of funds. As such, it can be useful for purchases and donations where privacy is desired. Unfortunately, it also often gets used for illicit activity – such as ransom demands and illegal drugs.

Finite supply

Whereas with traditional currencies, the total amount in circulation can be increased by the issuing government, Bitcoin has enforced scarcity, in that its source code limits the number of possible Bitcoin units to 21 million. (At the time of this writing, there are approximately 18.5 million Bitcoins that have been mined.) This concept of finite supply prevents inflation.

So with those stated advantages as a currency, there are some caveats which we will look at throughout this book.

Although some brick-and-mortar stores and eCommerce platforms accept Bitcoin as payment, many people are not primarily using it as a currency. Bitcoin is viewed primarily as an **investment** for most people. They are treating it more like stocks or real estate – something they can buy that they anticipate will go up in value.

Bitcoin started out with no "value". But value needed to be contributed (in the form of computational power) in order to "mine" Bitcoin. (More on that in the next chapter.) Thus, while Bitcoin has no inherent value, people needed to invest computational resources in order to obtain Bitcoin. And the resources required has steadily increased as more Bitcoin are mined.

As with anything of a finite supply in a free market, the more people want it, the higher the price those that have it can charge for it. Take seats in a sports stadium – there is a limited number of seats.

If a lot of people want to watch a game (such as the Superbowl), then the NFL will raise the price to the maximum that they can charge and fill the stadium. There are likely millions of people that would buy Superbowl tickets for $10. But if the stadium only holds 80,000, then they can only sell 80,000 tickets. If they charged $50,000 per ticket, they might only sell 1,000 tickets. But if they charge $5,000 a ticket, they will likely fill the stadium. While there are many factors - and obviously in this case they can also charge more for better seats – there is a limited supply, and only so much that people will pay. Fundamentally, this principle is called the law of supply and demand.

How does that apply to Bitcoin? Enforced scarcity – or in other words, a finite supply, that many people want to own. This drives the price up. There is no limit to what people may value Bitcoin at. If enough people want to invest in Bitcoin, the price depends on what other people are willing to sell it for. The price is only determined by what people are willing to pay – and as such, the price could potentially reach $1M and beyond. As there has been an opportunity to get rich quickly, particularly for early investors, many people hear of their success and want to "get in on it".

It has been said that there was a time when it literally cost 10,000 Bitcoin for 2 pizzas, and now 2 Bitcoin would buy you 10,000 pizzas.

With many concerned about inflation and government overreach, Bitcoin is also seen by many as a form of financial security, independent from their local currency. To them, buying Bitcoin can be likened to buying precious metals like gold and silver.

In short, Bitcoin is seen by some as a replacement currency. For some it is seen as security. By some it is seen as an investment. And by others as a gamble, almost like buying lottery tickets. For others, it is simply a cool craze to be involved in. For many people buying Bitcoin, they are likely rationalizing it with several of these aspects.

Chapter 3: Understanding Blockchain Technology

"An investment in knowledge pays the best interest."

- Benjamin Franklin

Blockchain technology can have many applications, but the concept was originally formulated by its pseudonymous inventor, Satoshi Nakamoto, and published in a whitepaper in 2008 for the purpose of creating a decentralized cryptocurrency which he called Bitcoin.

While blockchain technology and Bitcoin are separate, for these purposes we are expressly looking at how Bitcoin employs blockchain technology.

The challenge the founder faced was to find a way to conduct financial transactions strictly via communication (over the internet) without any need for trust. With typical commerce, both parties wishing to exchange funds use a "trusted" third-party – such as a bank, which ensures that the holder of funds can only spend them once.

Fundamentally, a blockchain is simply a ledger of all transactions. In contrast to a bank, where transactions are non-public, this blockchain ledger is public to everyone. However, in order to maintain a level of privacy, there is pseudo-anonymity, in that there is no name published to identify an account number (or in Bitcoin terms, a wallet address). As such it is very difficult to identify the individuals or businesses transferring funds.

This "ledger" is recorded in a distributed database – that is, no one person or central server controls it. There are copies on thousands of computers (called nodes) around the world.

Every 'block' of transactions on the blockchain are independently verified by a multitude of these nodes (in a process known as 'mining') and become immutable. Subsequent blocks are chained together – each referencing the previous block. Thus how we get the term "blockchain".

Since the receiver does not necessarily trust the sender, and since there is no third-party arbitrating disagreements, there cannot be reversals – payments are final.

If you want to understand the technical aspects of the mining process, there are many resources explaining how Bitcoin works, and this is not intended to be an in-depth explanation. However, a brief summary as follows will likely satisfy the typical reader.

Essentially, the security of Bitcoin relies on the "proof of work" concept. Computing power is used to create a one-way cryptographic hash. These hashes are essentially impossible to reverse-engineer - thus why they are termed "one-way". As an example, you could input the word "hello" into the hashing equation, and it would provide a distinct hash. (Bitcoin uses SHA-256, so in this case, the hash of the word "hello" is: 2CF24DBA5FB0A30E26E83B2AC5B9E29E1B161E5C1FA7425E7304 3362938B9824) The same method/equation with the same input will always produce the same hash. But it is essentially impossible to take the hash of lengthy complex data and get the data in return from just the hash.

In Bitcoin, a hash is made of three primary entries: the transactional details of the new block, the hash of the previous block in the chain, along with a nonce. A nonce is an arbitrary value (number or characters / bit string) used to provide uniqueness in cryptography. It must find a nonce which when hashed along with the aforementioned, results in a hash meeting certain characteristics. (Such as starting with nineteen zero bits.) This takes considerable computing power, in that typically trillions of hashes will be generated trying to find a hash that meets the required characteristics. (For the technical readers, since the nonce size is limited to 32 bits, there are things that can be altered beyond just the nonce, including the "coinbase", timestamp, etc. – but that is beyond the scope of this summary.)

The first mining node to find a valid hash thus "locks in" the details of the transactions with their corresponding timestamps. In the completed block, each transactional record perpetually documents that the transaction between two addresses took place at a given time, since that hash could not have been generated without having known the details. The completed block and its hash (and how it was arrived at) are then shared on the peer-to-peer network with the other Bitcoin nodes to in turn verify, and then they start working on the next block.

In order to compensate for the computational power (which is the "proof of work" fundamentally required to maintain Bitcoin), the successful mining nodes ("miners") are "issued" Bitcoin (and transaction fees) as a reward for their work of closing a block. This is the only way that new Bitcoin are issued.

The Bitcoin software is designed to vary the difficulty of the required characteristics of the resulting hash, dependent on how many nodes are actively mining, and how powerful the computer hardware is, in order to maintain that a block is closed approximately every 10 minutes. As such, the more Bitcoin miners there are, the more energy it takes to mine the same number of Bitcoins.

In regard to its software-specified controlled release, the amount of Bitcoin awarded for closing a block halves every 4 years, and the last Bitcoin is projected to be mined in 2140.

Again, this is not intended to be an in-depth look at all the nuances of blockchain technology or its application with Bitcoin, but rather to simply provide a basic understanding of its core concept.

Chapter 4: The Software is Key

"The trouble with programmers is that you can never tell what a programmer is doing until it's too late."

- Seymour Cray

Bitcoin software is open-source. For the less technical reader, that means that anyone can view the source code. This is different from conventional commercial software, such as Apple's iOS, for instance, where only specific Apple employees are provided access to the source code.

Open-source also typically means that developers from around the world can contribute to the software – suggest tweaks, fix bugs, and create new features or enhancements.

The community of developers involved in various open-source software projects generally create excellent software. Instead of a small team working for a particular company, there can be dozens of people contributing to a given piece of software.

Much of the software you use every day (without even realizing it) has been provided by developers contributing to open source. As an example, Wordpress, a website management platform that by some estimates is the backend for over 1/3 of all websites, is open-source. There are many other open-source web technologies such as Bootstrap, jQuery, Angular, React, etc. that are used by countless websites, including the likes of Google, YouTube, Facebook, Instagram, Twitter, Amazon, and nearly every other online service you may use. And nearly all the servers hosting these platforms will be running a Linux-based open-source operating system. Chances are that every website you have visited has been made possible by open-source software.

As such, this is certainly not an attempt to bash contributors to open-source software. Many of them are diligent and principled.

However, open-source only works if there is no combined malicious intent. At the time of this writing, there are fewer than 50 people actively involved in maintaining the Bitcoin software code base.

As such, this is a potential Bitcoin Defect. Let me explain a few potential scenarios.

Scenario A: Infiltration

Consider if a major nation wanted to stop Bitcoin. We will use the United States as an example. If the Federal Reserve decided that Bitcoin was a threat to the trust and stability of the US Dollar, they could get hundreds of federal agents (CIA / NSA / FBI / DoD CC / etc.), to work on Bitcoin development. These undercover developers / agents could work to provide legitimate tweaks for months. And then one could slip in some obscure code to a core section, and a few dozen other "developers" could approve the commit to the master repository. Most likely that code would not take effect until a particular trigger occurred – a certain date reached, a certain transaction, a certain fluctuation, etc. But it would act like a ticking time bomb. It could be delayed until perhaps a year later, by which time most of the Bitcoin miners had updated to the latest version.

What could this code do? It is unlikely that the "implanted virus" would be designed to simply halt all activity. But for instance, it could be altered to start "randomly" hijacking transactions – where Bitcoin is moved to an address other than the intended address. Or it could be designed to designate some addresses invalid, so that existing wallets were no longer accessible. Or it could stop awarding new Bitcoins and transaction fees to miners, in which case they would stop mining. Or it could dramatically increase transaction fees to users. If the source-code of ANY software is in control of those with malicious intent, it can be altered in any number of different ways. No doubt the goal would be to create chaos and loss of trust, rather than to technically bring the entire network down. Dismantling a global peer-to-peer network is difficult even for a major government, but even an amateur can create chaos. Essentially, you could think of this as software terrorism or cyber war – but war on a competing financial system vs. war on a nation. Frankly – and I am not trying to start a conspiracy here - we would likely never know if any of the current Bitcoin developers are already funded by the US Government (or another nation) in some indirect manner.

Scenario B: Bribes

Similar to the above scenario, a major government could most likely bribe existing developers working on Bitcoin to achieve their purposes. If a government felt Bitcoin was a major threat to it solely controlling the financial situation in their country, they could bribe a couple dozen Bitcoin developers and get through any code they wanted. And while I am sure many of the Bitcoin developers are principled and could not be bribed, you cannot convince me that many of them would not accept a bribe. If offered $100 Million each – enough to buy a private plane, fancy sports cars, a nice yacht, a waterfront estate on a Caribbean island, and to never need to work a day job again in their lives – you will have a hard time convincing me that none of them can be bribed. Yet that would cost only a few billion dollars, a drop in the bucket for many major nations.

Scenario C: Advanced Malware

Another potential avenue is the ability for mining computers to be compromised for malicious intent. A number of nations have extremely advanced methods for creating and infiltrating computer systems. Take for instance the widespread hack of Solar Winds in 2020. (If you have not heard of it, Solar Winds is an Information Technology management platform, used by thousands of major companies and government agencies. It was a very sophisticated attack that flew under the radar for many months and provided attackers with ample access to systems.) Even aside from nations, there are many independent hacking groups with significant experience in compromising systems, creating viruses, distributing ransomware, etc.

In such a scenario, the official core Bitcoin software repository does not change, but if the hackers are successful in compromising a majority of mining nodes (granted, a large number), they could develop a virus which could alter the Bitcoin software these nodes are running, which in turn could create havoc, in ways similar to mentioned in scenario A. Of necessity, these computers are all connected to the internet, and thus are always potentially at risk of being hacked.

You might think that none of the scenarios in this chapter could happen. Or you might think that they could happen, but that it would be short term. But something is only worth what people trust it to be worth. Remember the Enron scandal – once something loses people's trust, it is very difficult to regain it. If people were to stop trusting the security of Bitcoin, it would be only logical for them to try to cash out, and as more and more people decided to cut their losses, its value would dramatically collapse. Since any currency is based on trust, erosion of that trust creates a fragile system.

Chapter 5: The China Factor

"There's no trust system in China."

- Jack Ma

You may ask, what does a certain country have to do with Bitcoin? Well, in China's case, quite a bit. Frankly, over the last few decades, Chinese products have achieved a near monopoly in many markets. Chances are high that the components in your smartphone and your computer are mostly or entirely manufactured in China. And guess what - so are the specialized computers that are used for mining Bitcoin.

In China, companies mining Bitcoin have nearby access to the latest and most powerful mining systems – thereby avoiding shipping costs and delays. They also have access to a bright and inexpensive workforce of technicians. And perhaps most importantly, access to cheap electricity.

As such, it might come as little surprise that China currently mines over 60% of all Bitcoin. (Or in more technical terms, its mining pools have over 60% of the worldwide Bitcoin hashrate.) In comparison, no other country currently exceeds 10% - there has been a huge centralization of Bitcoin mining in China.

Somewhat ironically, in recent years the government of China – through the Chinese Communist Party (CCP) control of the People's Bank of China (PBOC) - has banned its citizens from using Bitcoin (or other cryptocurrencies).

In China, the government controls just about everything. This is crucial to understand. While some degree of "capitalism" is allowed, essentially all companies in China operate at the permission of the CCP and can be forced to do the government's bidding.

Hereby China has no fewer than three major factors by which they exert a large degree of control over Bitcoin:

1) Prohibiting its legal use in China
2) Hardware manufacturing
3) The Blockchain 51% rule

Prohibited

By banning the use of Bitcoin in China, Bitcoin loses legal access to approx. 1.4 Billion people, and a major business economy on the global scale – perhaps the single largest by some measures, and an incredibly important trading partner to nearly every nation on earth.

So far Beijing has allowed most mining facilities to continue operating in China – but they have ample options to hinder that within their country as well – such as blocking their internet connections or cutting off their electricity. The global Bitcoin network would be resilient to such national interference though.

Hardware

China could also ban the manufacturing of mining hardware, which while not a defect, could impact Bitcoin over the longer term.

Since the Chinese government can control the companies producing nearly all the Bitcoin mining hardware, which nodes are essential to not just producing more Bitcoin, but also confirming the transactions on the blockchain; it conceivably could introduce firmware-level malware which could render Bitcoin useless, similar to what was outlined in the last chapter from a software standpoint.

The 51% Rule

This is perhaps the most concerning; per the original whitepaper outlining Bitcoin (https://bitcoin.org/bitcoin.pdf), authored by Satoshi Nakamoto over a decade ago, he notes in the abstract how the security of the system is dependent on there never being a majority of CPU power in the network attempting a coordinated attack:

> "As long as a majority of CPU power is controlled by nodes that are not cooperating to attack the network, they'll generate the longest chain and outpace attackers."

And he further states in the Introduction:

> "The system is secure as long as honest nodes collectively control more CPU power than any cooperating group of attacker nodes."

In his original concept, Bitcoin was designed to be very decentralized. And although it largely is, there is a notable exception. The majority of the Bitcoin hash rate is executed in China – and by a wide margin. The mining nodes themselves may be spread across China – but like everything in China, they are all ultimately controlled by a very centralized government.

People in China that do not do the government's bidding tend to be demoted - or disappear entirely. Chinese citizens have a very strong incentive to follow the direction of the CCP.

Because the majority of the processing power supporting Bitcoin is in China, this could be capitalized on by Chinese authorities that wish to end Bitcoin – in favor of China's own digital currency. They could launch an attack on Bitcoin by falsifying the blockchain. Such a hack, if executed correctly, could eliminate people's Bitcoin holdings by transferring them to wallets owned by the CCP.

This is an inherent defect in the design of Bitcoin – one that the original developer knew of - but he apparently did not envision the ability for a communist regime to achieve control over the majority of the network's CPU power.

Chapter 6: Environmental Impact

"There is nothing more frightful than ignorance in action."

- Johann Wolfgang von Goethe

Many people have raised concerns about the environmental impact of Bitcoin mining. Let us consider whether this is valid. Obviously, we should be careful not to destroy the planet we live on. For the sake of our children and future generations, it is our duty to take care of Earth. While I do not consider myself to be an environmentalist, pollution and needless waste of resources disgusts me. (And I should clarify, by pollution here I am referring to toxic chemicals, trash, and smog – not carbon dioxide which plants require to grow.) Most of what passes for "science" these days is politically motivated and funded, with little basis in the fundamentals of scientific theory and practice – but that is another matter.

Electricity

Computing the proof of work in Bitcoin mining certainly uses a lot of electricity; it has been estimated at consuming over $1/200^{th}$ of the entire world's electricity usage. Global Bitcoin mining nodes currently use more electricity than the entire usage of many individual countries.

Much of this electricity is generated around the world with natural gas or petroleum products, and in China, they have recently been substantially increasing their use of coal in electricity generation.

There are many "green energy" initiatives to provide cleaner, more sustainable energy – but these are fairly insignificant compared to global energy use. And often the total environmental effect of producing and maintaining solar panels and wind turbines is less "friendly" than the forms of energy they replace. Seeing pictures of hundreds of decommissioned wind turbine blades being buried, or the electronic waste of expired solar panels, forces one to recognize how there is more than just the operation that must be accounted for in regard to the total environmental effect. Hydroelectric dams are relatively "green", but there are limited areas conducive to building dams. Believe it or not, properly managed nuclear energy is one of the most sustainable and environmentally friendly forms of generating electricity. There are also developments being made to harness wave and tidal energy – although the long-term cost effectiveness of such mechanisms in ocean salt water is questionable; and a lot of people do not live near the coast. It is also possible we will see substantially more efficient solar panels and battery technology developed in the future, which will negate many of the detrimental effects of current wind and solar equipment and allow them to truly be more sustainable and effective.

You may wonder how this really matters in a conversation about Bitcoin. I think the environmental question is important to understand; and while it can be dismissed, should not be done so without weighing the situation. Currently very little Bitcoin mining would take place using only non-subsidized "green energy" – it simply would not be cost effective at current Bitcoin prices. Those calling for Bitcoin to "go green" do not fully understand the consequences.

From another perspective however, the total energy used in gold mining each year rivals that of Bitcoin. Many people have called Bitcoin "digital gold" – so if it lived up to its name, the electricity use is perhaps justified. Although we must also remember that gold has many uses in manufacturing, etc. besides just a store of value.

Some have estimated that the combined banking systems around the world also consume more electricity than Bitcoin mining does. Which is perhaps more of a fair comparison than mining gold, although the number of people who use banks vastly exceeds those with Bitcoin, since currently far less than 1% of the world's population have even a dollar worth of Bitcoin.

Perhaps for proponents of Bitcoin, the best justification could be that nations go to great lengths militarily to protect their currency, economies, and financial interests. In an "altruistic world", if this could be largely avoided because of a mathematically based system of currency and trust, the electricity requirements would be well worth it. Believe what you will about that – I am not holding my breath.

Hardware obsolescence

In the early days of Bitcoin, you could use your own computer's CPU to mine Bitcoin. After a while, people found that GPU chipsets were considerably faster. Now however, nearly all Bitcoin mining is performed by application-specific integrated circuit (ASIC) units – typically with hundreds of such units housed in a data center. While the hardware might physically last for 5 years, as technology progresses, eventually it is no longer profitable to run outdated technology. If other miners have the updated technology, you will spend more in electricity than you will reap in Bitcoin reward. As such, the old units will eventually be discarded as electronic waste.

With cryptocurrency like Bitcoin, once someone else has a substantially faster mining unit, a slower unit becomes essentially valueless. As an example, perhaps you had a mining rig that had been generating an average of $50 worth of Bitcoin per day while using $25 per day of electricity. Then other people get faster mining rigs, so after a while you find that you are now only averaging $25 worth of Bitcoin per day while still using $25 per day of electricity. At that point you decide to replace it. Of course, this issue is not strictly limited to just Bitcoin – the servers used by Google, Facebook, etc. also have a limited lifespan. But unlike Bitcoin, normal web servers and computers can typically still handle the same workloads they did a year prior – the value the computing power provides typically far exceeds the cost of the electricity for many years.

With each major upgrade in computer technology, many tons of Bitcoin mining computer hardware will be discarded, since it will no longer be financially viable to continue operating it. This has obvious environmental consequences, as most of this hardware – particularly in less developed countries – is unlikely to be recycled, and the toxic waste will over time contaminate the environment.

While the environmental concern is not a "defect" of Bitcoin, it is an effect of Bitcoin, and I anticipate this being used by governments and the media to condemn the use of Bitcoin. This is not a matter of a single flaw, but of many cards being stacked against its continued success.

Chapter 7: Quantum Computing

"The disruptive potential of quantum technology will make the change of the Internet era look like a small bump in the road!"

- Kevin Coleman

BITCOIN DEFECT

Quantum computing is an emerging technology. I start this chapter with a disclaimer – I by no means consider myself an expert in the intricacies of quantum computing. However, my lack of understanding does not negate that experts in this field are anticipating the viability of a major leap in certain types of computing power in the next few years. This could have major ramifications for Bitcoin and other cryptocurrencies. (In addition to many other aspects of cryptographic security.)

What is quantum computing?

In conventional computer processors, a "bit" can be one of two states – 0 or 1, on or off. Thus we use the term binary. Our minds can fairly easily comprehend this, because similar to a light switch, it can be one of two states - on or off. We can understand digital, and we would also have little trouble understanding a switch or dial that could have multiple states – say ten different positions. We can also conceive a dial or lever that has an "infinite" number of positions that could be continuously variable – essentially what we refer to as "analog".

However, in quantum computer processors, it is not "analog", but not really "digital" either. In quantum technology, a bit is referred to as a qubit – and it also can be 0 or 1 – but it has the unique aspect that it can also be BOTH 0 AND 1 simultaneously. As such, it can handle uncertainty in ways conventional computers cannot. While baffling, it provides some extraordinary functionality when properly harnessed, and quantum computers can do certain calculations exponentially faster than conventional computers.

Currently quantum computers are still experimental – they are large delicate units that are not all that reliable and typically need to be kept at frigid temperatures. Perhaps a good comparison of their current state is like computers in the 1940's (such as Colossus or ENIAC), which used vacuum tubes in the days prior to transistors.

In 2019, Google claimed to achieve what they refer to as Quantum Supremacy – that is, their experimental quantum computer was able to perform calculations they claim would overwhelm a conventional supercomputer. It is not just theory anymore.

Engineers working at Google's Santa Barbara quantum technology research facility estimate a quantum computer will be able to perform calculations in about 3 minutes what would take the fastest non-quantum conventional supercomputer 10,000 years. Different researchers have different perspectives, and time will tell how this unfolds.

Besides Google, there are many other companies working on quantum computing, including many of the major technology players - such as IBM, Microsoft, Intel, HP – along with some lesser-known companies such as D-Wave and IonQ. While the technology is still in relative infancy and it will be quite some time (if ever) before you have a quantum processor in your laptop or smartphone, the computational possibilities are phenomenal.

How does this affect Bitcoin?

Considering that Bitcoin is designed such that the last Bitcoin is expected to be mined in the year 2140 – what is the chance that

Bitcoin will even be relevant a couple decades from now with the onset of quantum computing?

Bitcoin was ingeniously designed, but like anything, when a new technology totally changes the game, it has many ramifications.

With Bitcoin (and many other uses of asymmetric cryptography commonly used for security online), you have a private key and a public key, which have a mathematical relationship. Your private key can be used to generate a digital signature which in turn is validated with your public key. This type of authentication secures everything from online shopping, to your Bitcoin wallet.

Currently, with the computing power of today's conventional computers, it is essentially impossible to derive the private key from a public key. Depending on the type of encryption, it would take a phenomenally long time (hundreds of years) to crack.

But if you have a quantum computer that can use certain algorithms in a far more powerful manner that can derive the private key from the public key, then your digital signature can be forged, and the once unbreakable security vanishes.

The first aspect of how Bitcoin is susceptible to this are old wallet addresses using p2pk and reused p2pkh addresses for which the public key is available; it is estimated that there are several million Bitcoin currently that fall into this category. Provided these are moved to unused p2pkh addresses before the quantum computers are able to crack their private keys, it is thought these would be secure against this sort of attack. (Currently these could be susceptible if a quantum computer could derive a private key from a public key in a matter of perhaps a few months.)

A fundamentally more detrimental flaw would occur if quantum computers become powerful enough to derive a private key from a public key in under 10 minutes. At that point, widescale theft of Bitcoins could occur at any transaction, and the Bitcoin blockchain technology would have to be fundamentally redesigned to employ quantum-resistant cryptography.

I frankly do not expect quantum computing to be the demise of Bitcoin – I expect it to all but disappear sooner than that. But I could be wrong, in which case quantum technology could prove to be a major defect for Bitcoin as we know it in the coming decades.

Chapter 8: Traceability and Totalitarianism

*"Who controls the past controls the future.
Who controls the present controls the past."*

- George Orwell

World leaders enjoy the prestige and wealth of their positions. Throughout history the ruling class has tried to maintain a firm grip on their power – understandably so – and except for a few exceptions, they only relinquish their power upon defeat or at their death.

In the past century, we have encountered circumstances somewhat unique in history, in that nations have willingly bestowed some of their authority to global or regional organizations. The formation of the United Nations, or that of the European Union, is different from the empires of ancient Egypt, Babylon, or that of the Greeks and Romans. These controlled vast regions, but they conquered their territories - or by overwhelming military superiority, forced their surrender.

With each passing generation, the power of the modern global leaders is increasing. Whether through the UN itself, or through "subsidiaries" (in the broad sense) such as the World Economic Forum (WEF), International Criminal Court (ICC), International Monetary Fund (IMF), World Bank Group, and even the likes of the World Health Organization (WHO). These globalists want the power to control you.

One of the best ways to control you is by controlling the currency you use. Just think how governments use interest rates, inflation, taxes, and tax credits to manipulate the behavior of their citizens to achieve their desired results. Inevitably, eventually Bitcoin will obstruct their purposes, and sooner or later will be increasingly banned. For the time being, these globalists are quite happy to have Bitcoin change your mindset and opinion of digital global currency. Most people who have used Bitcoin will be accustomed to the concepts behind digital currency – so essentially, right now Bitcoin is working to help eventual adoption. That is no fault of Bitcoin, but my assumption of why it is permitted by many governments and becoming more mainstream.

At this point, many governments are in the research phase of exploring digital currency. A few countries have pilot projects underway. Digital payments are convenient. However, unlike Bitcoin, national (or global) digital currencies will be fully controlled by those in power.

Using a social credit system like China has been rolling out, every choice and purchase you make will be tracked – and may be denied. (China has already denied tens of millions of people from traveling.) As we have seen how many freedoms were wiped out so quickly in the name of collective health in 2020, it should come as little surprise for the rest of the world to follow China's lead with their own systems in the near future.

As if it were not enough that the major governments of the world are pushing in this direction, the ways we interact and share information are becoming increasingly controlled by a few major players. The "Big Tech" companies including Google, Facebook, Twitter, Microsoft, Apple, Amazon, and others are nearly all politically aligned with eliminating separate nations in favor of a globally connected world. Expect them all to support digital currencies in the near future; any embrace of Bitcoin *(or at least*

Bitcoin as we know it) will be temporary. We have seen how many of these companies are quite willing to provide censorship of information, and there is little reason to believe they would act any differently if they could be involved in controlling your actions with currency.

Bitcoin ultimately does not serve their purposes of control. Interest rates and inflation cannot be controlled in the same way as a fiat government currency. Transactions have pseudo-anonymity – a core feature of Bitcoin - which makes selective taxation difficult and is not conducive to be easily connected to a social credit system.

For similar reasons, many governments are gradually trying to phase out cash money. Paper bills are difficult to trace, and transactions in cash are less likely to be taxed. (There is also of course the issue of counterfeiting.) Digital payments are far more easily traced, and algorithms can be applied across millions of transactions to automatically determine actions being taken that the government does not approve of, and then those individuals can be identified.

In addition to environmental concerns discussed in a previous chapter, crime is a major factor likely to be publicly communicated by governments eventually wishing to ban Bitcoin. While certainly not the predominate use of Bitcoin, an anonymous transfer of funds is highly desirable by criminals involved in drugs, ransomware, and human trafficking. Even when it comes to cash, there are continually more banking regulations aimed at avoiding fraud and money laundering. I will not be surprised to see cash phased out as well.

With much of the mainstream media either being directly controlled and/or funded by governments, or at least ideologically aligned with their purposes - do not be surprised if the media promotes the notion that any privacy in transactions must be eliminated.

While Bitcoin is designed with no central controls, consider for a moment how it can be banned in practice. If the United Nations / World Economic Forum / International Monetary Fund, etc. issued a mandate that Bitcoin needed to be stopped, many countries where Bitcoin is currently legal would likely adopt a ban. A few major governments could declare ownership, transactions, development, and mining of any cryptocurrency an illegal activity. They could provide a short amnesty period, where perhaps they would allow conversion to their own digital currency. (Even at 50 cents on the dollar, many people would go along with that to avoid issues with the law.) After a short time, no doubt the media would align anyone involved in Bitcoin as not just doing something illegal but as a "terrorist". Keep in mind, that while currently Bitcoin is mostly allowed in the western hemisphere, there are already numerous countries around the world that have banned Bitcoin and other crypto currencies partially or entirely, and where transacting in Bitcoin as a citizen is illegal. A quick internet search should provide you an up-to-date list.

If Bitcoin became illegal in most parts of the world, its value would plummet – many people could not legally use it, and even for those who could, a large degree of trust would be lost in the system by people whose Bitcoin "assets" had dropped to very little value.

Chapter 9: Prophetic Viewpoint

"In twenty-five years, the Bible will be a forgotten book."

- Robert Ingersoll (1833 – 1899)

When you and I make predictions, they are just guesses. If we are well versed on the subject, they might be educated guesses, and the probability of them coming to pass might increase, but they are nevertheless still subject to often being wrong. No stock market investor always makes a profit, no matter how well they understand their investments and the market. No advisor or general always has the best plan of action. People simply cannot accurately predict the future.

The quote on the previous page is a prime example. Robert Ingersoll has been dead for well over a century, yet time has shown his prediction to have been proved blatantly wrong. Countless others have made similar predictions over the centuries.

Yet, in 2020, numerous online bookstores actually reported <u>record</u> sales of Bibles. It is estimated that there are approximately 100 million copies of the Bible printed each year, and that is just in paper form. There are many Bible apps, and just the YouVersion Bible app alone has over 400 million downloads.

That goes to show how arrogant someone can be to predict the downfall of something. There were also prominent people who predicted that telephones, television, and automobiles were just fads.

As such, while I see several glaring defects with Bitcoin, as outlined in the prior chapters, perhaps my own reasoning is wrong; why would I venture to predict its demise? That is because I trust the Author of the Bible, and the Bible has much to say about future events. While we mere humans cannot accurately predict the future, the God of the Bible holds the future in His hands.

You may say you do not believe in a God who knows more than you. You may think there is no Higher Power. You may think your life and that of all of mankind came about purely by chance, and thus has no ultimate purpose. You may think the Bible is just stories, and that it is silly to have any confidence in a book written thousands of years ago. You may think it irrelevant – and that you would never place blind trust in an ancient book.

You may be unaware, however, that there are many good reasons to have faith in the Bible – it certainly need not be blind trust. The Bible has been proven correct time and time again in the areas of science (through modern advances), history (through archaeological discoveries), and foretelling the future (through fulfilled prophecies). Even though the common knowledge of the day (in some cases even for thousands of years) was something different, the Bible, the Word of God, held the truth all along. The Bible is not shy about God knowing the future, for He is outside of time itself:

> But there is a God in heaven that revealeth secrets, and maketh known to the king Nebuchadnezzar what shall be in the latter days. (Daniel 2:28a, KJV)

> I am Alpha and Omega, the beginning and the ending, saith the Lord, which is, and which was, and which is to come, the Almighty. (Revelation 1:8, KJV)

The Bible contains about 2,500 prophesies, around four-fifths of which have already been accurately fulfilled throughout history. The remaining approximately 500 prophesies are to do with the future. There are many books and articles written about these – both pointing to the accuracy of fulfillment, and outlining prophesies yet to be fulfilled before the end of the world. It is beyond the scope of this book to outline these in detail, but I encourage you to investigate Bible prophesy if you are unfamiliar.

The Bible foretells that in the future, the nations of the world will all rally behind a single global leader. This leader will control virtually all aspects of the global economy and affairs. Here is the prophesy:

> And he causeth all, both small and great, rich and poor, free and bond, to receive a mark in their right hand, or in their foreheads: And that no man might buy or sell, save he that had the mark, or the name of the beast, or the number of his name. (Revelation 13:16-17, KJV)

Now I agree this does not entirely preclude Bitcoin from potentially being a form of payment in that day – but the very essence of Bitcoin is designed to facilitate non-centralized payments. And yet the Bible predicts entirely totalitarian global control. Picture someone coming to power - being the ruler of the entire world, with a level of control such that nobody could buy or sell without their mark – do you think they would make Bitcoin the de facto global currency? Any logical analysis would conclude that a global digital currency that was entirely centralized and traceable would suit the purposes of such a ruler much better.

Chapter 10: Conclusion

"He who dares not offend cannot be honest."

- Thomas Paine

Bitcoin has had an incredible following. Many people, from working-class to ultra-rich, see Bitcoin as a solution to many of our countries' financial woes, at least on a personal level. Like many others, I also see the economy flirting with calamity. As outlined in the first chapter, inflation resulting from unchecked spending and continual increases in money supply is an unnerving scheme.

I feel many of those who are investing in Bitcoin are concerned about losing a substantial portion of the buying power of their hard-earned savings to inflation. However, upon analyzing Bitcoin, I do not feel it would be prudent to invest in it – it has too many potential defects. I would not fault someone for using it as a currency while it lasts. Nor do I concern myself with warning the greedy gamblers or the ultra-rich who dabble in Bitcoin.

But for those with very limited resources, who see the proverbial "writing on the wall" in regard to the economy, and want to "do something", I write this book as a caution that Bitcoin is not without fault, and encourage you to evaluate the risks for yourself.

You may read this book, and say, "yeah, there are some risks, but I think it is still safer than fiat currency." That is fine, when you are aware of the risks. But for those who have put every spare cent into Bitcoin, thinking it is a safe investment that will only keep increasing in value, beware that it could collapse.

I do not venture to say *when* Bitcoin as we know it will end; I have no idea. It might be a dramatic collapse or a gradual waning. It could well become worth 10 times its current value before then.

As you will have noticed, this is not an expensive hard cover book stuffed with fluff. I aim to expose the risk, make my point, and let you do your own research. I have not provided footnotes as many links become quickly out of date. You can verify most of what I write, and find much more detail, with a quick online search.

Finally, I would like to thank you, the reader, for taking an interest in this subject and educating yourself as to the risks involved.

> A prudent man foreseeth the evil, and hideth himself; but the simple pass on, and are punished. (Proverbs 27:12, KJV)

www.ingramcontent.com/pod-product-compliance
Lightning Source LLC
Chambersburg PA
CBHW071123240526
45465CB00023B/783